Quality Assurance

By Solis Tech

Software Quality Assurance Made Easy

2nd Edition

Quality Assurance (2nd Edition): Software Quality Assurance Made Easy!

Table Of Contents

Quality Assurance (2nd Edition): Software Quality Assurance Made Easy!

Introduction

I want to thank you and congratulate you for purchasing the book, *"Quality Assurance: Software Quality Assurance Made Easy"*.

This book contains proven steps and strategies on how to implement Software Quality Assurance.

Software quality assurance evolved from the quality assurance in industrial production in the 1940s. With the introduction of computers and the development of applications, it has become an important aspect of software development. In this book, you will learn about the various concepts of software quality assurance and its application in your workplace.

Chapter 1 talks about the definitions of software quality assurance and quality control. It is necessary that you understand what it is so that you can fully grasp the other fundamental concepts. Chapters 2, 3, and 4 discuss the three software quality assurance models, namely the Capability Maturity Model Integration, the Six Sigma Model, and the ISO 90003 Model.

Chapter 5 talks about various activities of software quality assurance while Chapter 6 discusses the Software Quality Assurance Plan. Chapter 7 talks about Software Reliability Testing. Chapter 8 discusses the ways you can implement software quality assurance in an existing environment.

In Chapter 9, you will learn how you can ensure that the software produces quality outputs. Chapter 10 teaches you how to develop and run software testing while Chapter 11 talks about the timing of the software release. In Chapter 12, you will learn about using automated testing tools.

Thanks again for purchasing this book, I hope you enjoy it!

Chapter 1: Definition Of Software Quality Assurance And Software Testing

Software quality assurance is part of the process of software development. It includes the improvement and monitoring of the process. It also follows the processes, procedures, and standards. Furthermore, it ensures the resolution of problems discovered. In effect, it focuses on the prevention of problems.

Software testing, on the other hand, includes the operation of the application or system under controlled conditions, which must include all abnormal and normal conditions. The primary goal of software testing is to know what can go wrong when unexpected and expected scenarios occur. Its focus is on the detection of problems.

Companies differ in assigning responsibilities for quality assurance and software testing. There are organizations that combine both responsibilities to a single person or group. However, it is also common to have various teams that combine developers and testers. Project managers lead such teams. The decision to either combine or separate responsibilities depends on the company's business structure and size. Human beings or machines can perform software testing.

Some projects do not require a group of testers. The need for software testing depends on the project's context and size, the development methodology, the risks, the developers' experience and skill, and other factors. For example, a short-term, low-risk, and small project with expert developers, who know how to use test-first development or thorough unit testing, may not require software test engineers.

In addition, a small or new IT company may not have a dedicated software testing staff even its projects have a need for it. It may outsource software testing or use contractors. It may also adjust its approach on project development and management by using either agile test-first development or more experienced programmers. An inexperienced project manager may use his developers to do their own functional testing or skip thorough testing all together. This decision is highly risky and may cause the project to fail.

If the project is a huge one with non-trivial risks, software testing is important. The use of highly specialized software testers enhances the ability of the project to succeed because different people with different perspectives can offer their invaluable contribution because they have stronger and deeper skills.

In general, a software developer focuses on the technical issues to make a functionality work. On the other hand, a software test engineer focuses on what can go wrong with the functionality. It is very rare to come across a highly effective technical person, who can do both programming and testing tasks. As such, IT companies need software test engineers.

There are various reasons why software may have bugs. First, there is no communication or miscommunication as to the application's requirements. Second, the software is very complex so an inexperienced individual may have a difficult time understanding the software application. In addition, the software may be a big one and includes big databases, data communications, security complexities, different remote and local web services, and multi-tier distributed systems.

Third, there are programming errors. Fourth, the requirements of the software change because the end-user requests for them. In some cases, this end-user may not be aware of the effects of such changes, which can result in errors. The staff's enthusiasm is affected. Continuous modification requirements are a reality. Quality assurance and software test engineers must be able to plan and adapt continuous testing to prevent bugs from affecting the software.

Fifth, time pressures can be difficult to manage. Mistakes often occur during crunch times. Sixth, people involved in the project may not be able to manage their own egos. Seventh, the code has poor documentation or design. It is difficult to modify and maintain codes that are poorly written or documented. Bugs can occur if IT companies do not offer incentives for developers to write maintainable, understandable, and clear codes. Most companies offer incentives when they are able to finish the code quickly. Eighth, the use of software development tools can also result to bugs.

How Quality Assurance Evolved

In 1946, the US Occupation Forces established the Quality Movement in Japan. The movement follows the research of W. Edwards Deming and the Statistical Process Control papers. The methods discussed by the research and papers pertained to industrial production. Each process of production has an output with a required specification and a verifiable main product. The Quality Control group measures the output at different production stages. It ensures that the output falls within the acceptable variances.

The Quality Assurance group does not part in the production process. It audits the process to ensure compliance with the established standards and guidelines. It gives its input for the continuous improvement of the process. In a manufacturing setup, it is easy to differentiate between quality assurance and quality control. These methods become the norm in manufacturing. Since they work in industrial production, they spawned the birth of software quality control and software quality assurance.

Quality Attributes of Software

Hewlett Packard's Robert Grady developed the common definition of the Software Quality Attributes. The FURPS model identified the following characteristics: functionality, usability, reliability, performance, and supportability (FURPS).

The functional attributes pertain to the features of the software. They answer the question about the purpose of the software instead of its use. The reason for the software's existence is different from the concerns about its reliability, look and feel, and security. The usability attributes are characteristics pertaining to user interface issues like consistency, interface aesthetics, and accessibility.

The reliability attributes include recoverability, accuracy, and availability of the system while performance attributes pertain to issues like startup time, recovery time, system response time, and information throughput. Supportability addresses issues like localizability, scalability, installation, configurability, compatibility, maintainability, adaptability, and testability. The FURPS model evolved into FURPS+ to include specification of constraints like physical, interface, implementation, and design constraints.

The Software Quality Control team tests the quality characteristics. The tests for usability and functionality occur during execution of the actual software. On the other hand, adaptability and supportability tests occur through code inspection. It is not the responsibility of the Software Quality Control or Software Quality Assurance to put the quality attributes into the software. The Software Quality Control team tests for the absence or presence of such characteristics while the Software Quality Assurance group ensures that each stakeholder follow the right standards and procedures during software execution.

In theory, the implementation of FURPS+ will overcome the problems caused by the software's intangible nature because the Software Quality Control team can measure each software attribute. For example, the amount of time it takes for programmers to fix a bug is a measure of supportability. To improve it requires the implementation of new coding standards.

The Software Quality Control group can inspect the code to ensure compliance with the coding standard while the Software Quality Assurance team can ensure that the quality control and programmer teams follow the right standards and process. It is the duty of the Software Quality Assurance group to collect and analyze the time spent on fixing the bug so that it can provide an input in terms of its usefulness to the process improvement initiative.

Chapter 2: The Capability Maturity Model Integration

CCMI is a program of process improvement and appraisal by Carnegie Mellon University. It is a requirement in most US government contracts, especially those projects related to software development. It can be a guide for process improvement in an organization, a division, or even a project. It defines the process maturity levels as Initial, Managed, and Defined.

At present, the Capability Maturity Model Integration has three areas, namely Product and Service Development, Service Establishment and Management, and Product and Service Acquisition. A framework guides organizations for improving or developing processes to meet business goals. Initially, CMMI was useful in software engineering but evolved into a more generalized model to include other areas of interest like acquisition of products and services, delivery of services, and development of hardware products.

History of CMMI

The goal of CMMI was to improve the use of maturity models by including various models into a framework. The project included members from the Carnegie Mellon Software Engineering Institute, government, and industry. The National Defense Industrial Association and the Office of the Secretary of Defense sponsored the project.

CMMI evolved from the capability maturity model. In November 2010, it released Version 1.3 to support Agile Software Development, alignment of representation, and improvements to maturity practices. It integrates various organizational functions, provides guidance for processes involving quality, sets improvement process goals, and offers a benchmark for evaluating present processes.

CMMI Representation

CMMI can be staged or continuous. A continuous representation allows users to focus on important processes to meet the immediate business goals of the organization. On the other hand, the staged representation provides a basis for comparing organizations and project maturity. It also offers a sequence of improvements.

CMMI Model Framework

CMMI has seventeen core process areas that are common in various areas of interest. These process areas are Causal Analysis and Resolution, Configuration

Management, Decision Analysis and Resolution, Integrated Project Management, Measurement and Analysis, Organizational Process Definition, Organizational Process Focus, Organizational Performance Management, Organizational Process Performance, Organizational Training, Project Monitoring and Control, Project Planning, Process and Productivity Quality Assurance, Quantitative Project Management, Requirements Management, Risk Management, and Supplier Agreement Management.

CMMI Appraisal

There is no certification in CMMI but appraisal. An organization can have a capability level or maturity level rating. Most organizations value the measurement of their progress through appraisal.

Appraisal can occur because the organization wants to compare its processes with CMMI best practices. The organization also wants to know in what areas it can improve. An appraisal is also a way to tell the organization's suppliers and customers that its processes are at par with CMMI best practices. It is also a way to meet the requirements of customers.

Appraisals are of three classes, depending on the organization's improvement opportunities and its comparison with the CMMI best practices. A Class A appraisal is a formal appraisal that can provide a level rating to an organization. The appraisal teams use an appraisal method and CMMI model to evaluate the organization. When the results are out, the organization can then plan its improvements.

CMMI Applications

According to Software Engineering Institute, an appraised organization experiences increases of performance in customer satisfaction, quality, productivity, schedule, and cost. The median increase varies from 14% for customer satisfaction to 62% for productivity. The CMMI model deals with the "what" instead of the "how" so it cannot guarantee increase in performance for all organizations.

Chapter 3: The Six Sigma Model

The Six Sigma Model consists of tools and techniques for improvement of processes. Bill Smith introduced this concept in 1986 while he was still with Motorola. Jack Welch used this as a business strategy in 1995 at General Electric. At present, various industrial sectors use the Six Sigma Model.

The Six Sigma Model improves the output quality of a process through identification and removal of the causes of defects. It also minimizes variability in the business and manufacturing processes. This model uses quality management methodologies and creates a special group of experts within the organization.

Every project adheres to a specific sequence of steps with defined value targets like reduce pollution, reduce cycle time of a process, reduce costs, increase profits, and increase customer satisfaction. The term Six Sigma came from a manufacturing statistical modeling of processes. A process can have a sigma rating to indicate its percentage of defect-free products.

The Doctrine of the Six-Sigma Model

The Six Sigma model asserts that process results will be stable and predictable through continuous efforts. It is possible to measure, control, analyze, and improve business and manufacturing processes. Furthermore, quality improvement is sustainable if the entire organization commits to it.

The Six Sigma model focuses on attaining quantifiable and measurable financial returns. Its emphasis is on passionate and strong management support and leadership. It is committed to decisions based on verifiable statistical methods and data, instead of guesswork and baseless assumptions.

The Six Sigma Methodologies

The Six Sigma Model has two methodologies, namely DMAIC and DMADV. DMAIC is for improving present business processes while DMADV is for creating new process designs or new product.

The DMAIC Methodology

DMAIC stands for Define, Measure, Analyze, Improve, and Control. The Define phase requires the definition of specific customer requirements, project goals, and the system itself. The Measure phase requires the collection of relevant data in order to measure the present process.

The Analyze phase investigates and verifies the data for cause-and-effect relationships. It tries to find the root cause of every defect discovered. The Improve phase, on the other hand, optimizes the present process by using techniques and standard work for future state process.

The Control phase ensures corrections to any deviations from the standard before such deviations can cause defects. It implements control systems and monitors the process continuously.

The DMADV Methodology

DMADV stands for Define, Measure, Analyze, Design, and Verify. The Define phase defines the goals of the design based on the business strategy and customer specifications. The Measure phase identifies the critical characteristics of quality. It measures risks, process capability of production, and product capabilities.

The Analyze phase includes analysis in order to create and design alternatives while the Design phase chooses the best alternative from the previous phase and improves on it. Lastly, the Verify phase implements the process, sets up pilot runs, and turns it over to the process owners.

Important Six Sigma Roles

The Executive Leadership consists of the organization's top management. These people create the vision for the implementation of Six Sigma. They empower other people with resources and freedom to search for ideas for improving processes and overcoming resistance to change.

Champions are from the upper management assigned by the Executive Leadership. They implement the Six Sigma within the organization. They are also mentors of Black Belts.

Master Black Belts are in-house Six Sigma coaches assigned by Champions. They spend all their time to the implementation of Six Sigma. They guide the Green Belts and Black Belts and help the Champions, as well. They ensure the consistent application of Six Sigma concepts in different departments and functions.

Black Belts apply the methodology to certain projects. They are under the Master Black Belts and spend all their time on Six Sigma. They focus on project implementation and are special leaders with special tasks.

Green Belts implement the Six Sigma methodology with other responsibilities. They work under the Black Belts.

Six Sigma Applications

Six Sigma methodologies are usually for large organizations. General Electric was able to generate $350 million savings in 1998 because of its Six Sigma implementation. However, Six Sigma is not suited for organizations with less than 500 employees. Smaller organizations can choose to implement some techniques and tools from Six Sigma.

Important Characteristics of Six Sigma Quality Assurance

The Six Sigma approach and methods are benchmarks for excellence. They raise the standards of quality by implementing a methodical management approach to quality. Testing is important to ensure that the products and services meet the customers' requirements and the desired standards.

The approach of the Six Sigma Green Belt ensures quality in production. It promises and delivers quality of products and services. By being consistent in delivering quality, the quality assurance office must ensure that each aspect of development is above par.

The Quality Assurance Officer

The Quality Assurance Officer ensures the quality of products and services by taking care of the whole quality assurance process in the software development cycle. His task is to maintain high standards and improve on the predetermined quality assurance standards.

The Quality Assurance Officer is also in charge of overseeing sales statistics to find out the reason for any possible drop in sales. It is his responsibility to ensure that all employees work towards achieving a common quality goal. It is also important for him to stay up-to-date with recent workshops, seminars, and product launches involving quality management in order to maintain the technical knowledge about quality assurance standards.

Chapter 4: The ISO 90003 Model

The ISO 90003 is a management standard for quality software products and services.

System Requirements and Guidelines

The Software Quality Assurance team identifies the processes that will compose the quality management system. It also describes the sequential structure, as well as the interaction of processes with each other. The team also implements, manages, and supports the quality system using effective processes. It improves the quality management system through effective monitoring, evaluation, and improvement of processes.

The Software Quality Assurance group also develops a quality management system for its documents, which describe the life cycle models, software processes, and the quality system itself. It prepares a manual that documents procedures, process interactions, and quality system scope.

The team also controls the documents. It approves and distributes the documents. In addition, it ensures that each stakeholder has his own copy of the correct version of documents. The group preserves the usability of updated quality documents. It also maintains quality records to prove effectiveness of operations.

Management Requirements and Guidelines

The Software Quality Assurance team must promote quality by promoting the need to meet customer and software product requirements. It must develop a system for quality management that will support the organization's quality policy and objectives. It must implement the system by providing resources and encouraging people to adhere to the quality system requirements. Lastly, it must aim to improve the system for quality management by performing regular reviews and providing resources to improve the quality management system.

The Software Quality Assurance group must be able to identify and meet customer requirements. In addition, it must be able to enhance customer satisfaction. The team must also define its quality policy that meets the organization's purpose. It must emphasize the need to meet such requirements and facilitate the creation of quality goals. It must also manage its quality policy by communicating it within the organization and reviewing it to ensure its suitability.

The Software Quality Assurance group must draft the quality objectives for all functional areas and organizational levels. It must plan, implement, and improve the quality management system. The team also documents and communicates the responsibilities and authorities. It appoints a management representative to oversee, report, and support the maintenance of the system to the management. It also ensures the establishment of communication processes within the organization.

The Software Quality Assurance team also reviews the quality management system to evaluate its effectiveness. It examines the review inputs and generates actions to improve effectiveness of the management system and the software products. It also acts to address any requirements for resources.

Resource Requirements and Guidelines

The Software Quality Assurance group provides quality resources by identifying the resources required to meet regulatory and customer requirements, as well as to support the quality management system. It must also ensure that it provides quality personnel with the right education, experience, training, and skills. The team must define the acceptable competence levels. It must determine the awareness and training needs of the organization.

The team must identify infrastructure requirements like facilities, software, and hardware needed to develop the software. In addition, it must identify the tools needed to develop, support, protect, and control the software. It must also provide and maintain such infrastructure and tools. Lastly, it must identify, implement, and manage the quality work environment.

Realization Requirements and Guidelines

The Software Quality Assurance team must plan the realization process of the software by identifying its quality requirements and objectives, realization requirements and needs, risk management requirements, and record keeping requirements. It must develop the documents, record keeping systems, and quality control methods for the product realization processes.

The group must also plan its work using life cycle models. It must plan and implement the quality management system on each software project. Furthermore, it must seek to control the customers' requirements by identifying the requirements the customers want, the requirements dictated by the use of the software, the requirements imposed by other agencies, and the requirements the organization wants.

The team must be able to plan the software design and development, and create procedures to control them. In addition, it must be able to control the purchasing process so that the products meet the requirements. The group must be able to provide service and manage production. It must be able to identify measuring and monitoring requirements to ensure that the software product meets the requirements.

Remedial Requirements and Guidelines

Software Quality Assurance includes the planning and implementation of remedial processes. It must be able to measure and monitor customer satisfaction by identifying correctly the methods used to meet the requirements of the customers. It must also perform internal audits regularly.

The team must also establish procedures for nonconforming software products. It must be able to analyze information in order to define the quality management requirements. It must collect system data to measure and monitor the suitability and effectiveness of the quality management system. Lastly, the group must be able to maintain quality and correct nonconformities. It must take steps to prevent possible nonconformities.

Chapter 5: Software Quality Assurance Activities

As a process of evaluation and adherence to standards and procedures, software quality assurance ensures that the software product conforms to the set procedures and standards throughout the software development life cycle.

The SQA activities include many large tasks like creation of quality management plan, software engineering techniques applications, formal technical reviews implementation, multi-tier testing strategy application, process adherence enforcement, change control, impact of change measurement, SQA audits, and record keeping and reporting.

Quality Management Plan

A quality management plan includes the software's quality aspects that need development. It aids in putting checkpoints throughout the software development process and tracks changes based on the results of the checkpoints. It is a live plan used throughout the software development life cycle.

Software Engineering

There are software engineering techniques that are useful for the software designer so that he can produce software with the highest quality. The software designer uses techniques like Facilitated Application Specification Techniques and interviews to gather information, then he estimates the project with techniques like Function Point estimation, Work Breakdown Structure, or Source Lines of Code estimation.

Formal Technical Reviews

A formal technical review assesses the design and quality of a software prototype. The technical staffs, who discuss the software's quality requirements, conduct it. Done during the early stage of development, the formal technical review detects errors and prevents them from passing to the end of the process that will require rework.

Multi-Tier Testing Strategy

Software testing is important in quality assurance because it helps detect bugs or errors. Unit testing, integration testing, and system level testing are strategies used by various IT organizations. A software developer can perform unit and integration testing while a software tester performs system and functional testing. In some cases, selected clients participate in the testing process through beta testing to help find errors before the software's final release to the market.

Process Adherence

Process adherence focuses on the need for the software to adhere to the quality procedures. It combines process monitoring and product evaluation. Process monitoring ensures adherence to appropriate steps in the product development. It monitors the software development processes by comparing the documented procedures and the actual steps. Product evaluation, on the other hand, ensures adherence to the product standards. It ensures that the software meets the requirements.

Controlling Change

In this activity, automated tools combine with human procedures to ensure that there is an existing mechanism to control change. This mechanism ensures software quality by having a formal procedure for requests for change. It also controls the impact of change and evaluates the nature of change. Controlling change is present stages of development and maintenance.

Impact of Change

In the Software Development Life Cycle, there must a procedure to measure and monitor change to ensure software quality. The measurement of software quality ensures proper estimation of costs and resource requirements. To control quality, it is important to measure the software's quality and compare it with the standards.

Software quality metrics measure the effectiveness of tools and techniques, product quality, and productivity of activities. They allow developers and managers to propose changes and monitor activities throughout the whole life cycle of the software. Furthermore, these people can also initiate corrections to software.

SQA Audits

SQA audits compare the software development process with the standard processes. It helps ensure maintenance of proper control over the documents in the development process. Audits help the developer perform and monitor his activities.

Record Keeping and Reporting

Record keeping and reporting keep information relevant to software quality assurance. This activity compiles review, change control, audits, and testing results, as well as the other activities for future reference.

Chapter 6: The Software Quality Assurance Plan

SQA plan includes all procedures to ensure a high standard of quality within the software development process. It compares the actual quality against the planned quality during the development process. The management usually acts appropriately if the actual quality does not meet the required level of quality.

The plan offers guidelines and framework for developers so that they can make the code maintainable and understandable. It provides procedures for planning, writing, designing, documenting, testing, maintaining, and storing software.

Steps to Create a Software Quality Assurance Plan

First, create the SQA plan.

Second, seek plan acceptance from management. It is important for management to participate in the process for the plan to be successful. The management must be responsible for the provision of all required resources to ensure software quality. Its level of commitment must be high so every affected department within the organization can easily approve the plan. After approval, the SQA plan then undergoes configuration control.

During the approval process, the management gives the SQA plan administrator control over software quality. Often, software developers usually take control of software quality. The management must be able to explain to its staff its views regarding software quality vis-à-vis the cost of the SQA plan. There must be a formal project estimate about costs so that the formal plan is both economic and with sense.

Third, seek development acceptance from the major users of the plan. Software development and maintenance staffs must agree to cooperate in order to implement the SQA plan successfully. The team members must commit to follow the plan after its acceptance.

The success of the implementation relies on the managers and team members involved in the software development. In small project teams, everyone must participate actively in developing the SQA plan. For larger projects, there must representatives from each group to draft the plan. Furthermore, these people must provide constant feedback to all team members so that the acceptance of the plan will be unanimous.

Fourth, plan for the SQA plan's implementation. The SQA plan requires resources so that the staff can plan, formulate, and draft it. The person responsible for its implementation must be able to access such resources. Furthermore, the management must commit to provide such resources and support the SQA plan. To allocate resources successfully, it must be aware of project risks that can prevent the implementation of the plan. It must ensure that the implementation of the SQA plan runs smoothly.

Lastly, implement the SQA plan. Execution requires the cooperation of all team members because it also needs proper monitoring. Auditing the SQA plan must follow a schedule so that the software development does not encounter problems and delays. The implementation team must set up audit points periodically at certain milestones or during the development process.

Sample SQA Plan Template

Preface

Document Conventions

This section includes standard conventions used in the SQA plan to provide explanations and instructions to users when updating the plan.

Record of Changes

This is the list of changes made on the SQA plan. It is important to update this table as needed for easy monitoring of changes.

*A - ADDED M - MODIFIED D - DELETED

VERSION NUMBER	DATE	NUMBER OF FIGURE, TABLE OR PARAGRAPH	A* M D	TITLE OR BRIEF DESCRIPTION	CHANGE REQUEST NUMBER

Table of Contents

List of Figures

List of Tables

Section 1: Purpose

This section defines the organization, the tasks and responsibilities of the SQA, as well as the guidelines and reference documents necessary to perform the activities. Furthermore, it must provide the conventions, practices, and standards used in performing the SQA activities, as well as the methodologies, techniques, and tools to support the activities. Lastly, it must provide the SQA reporting.

1.1 Scope

It includes the SQA activities necessary for the software's life cycle. Furthermore, it includes the SQA policy, function, and group participating in the SQA plan. In addition, it includes the plan's goal and procedures for the compliance of the performance and technical requirements.

1.2 Identification

This section includes the list of Continuous Integration of the project. The list must also include a brief description, purpose, and the name of team member responsible for it.

1.3 System Overview

This section includes the description and intended use of the software. Furthermore, it includes all the subsystems, Continuous Integration, and highlights of each subsystem.

1.4 Document Overview

This section identifies the procedures and organizations used for the SQA activities.

1.5 Relationship to Other Plans

This includes the evaluation of the SQA based on processes in the Software Development Plan. It establishes the criteria for the implementation procedures of the project.

1.6 Reference Documents

The list of reference documents is a part of this SQA plan.

Section 2: Management

This section includes every important element of the organization, which can influence software quality.

2.1 Organization

The SQA group must be independent if the Software Quality Assurance is to be successful. It must be able to elevate any problem with software quality to the management above the project level. Although it rarely happens, this reporting system to the upper management gives the SQA group the ability to resolve issues at the project level.

The functional groups that can influence software quality are program management, project management, system engineering, software design and development, software testing, system testing, logistics, software configuration management, independent verification and validation, and systems engineering process.

2.2 Resources

Resources include a list of equipment, facilities, and personnel necessary to implement software quality assurance.

Section 3: SQA Tasks

This section describes the software life cycle, the tasks, and the relationship of the tasks and the primary checkpoints. The tasks are in sequential order and must reflect verified tasks related to the software's activities.

The schedule of the tasks is also in this section. A task is complete if the required reports are also completed. Tasks can include review of software products, evaluation of software tools, evaluation of facilities, evaluation of the review process, etc.

Section 4: Documentation

This section describes and supports the software development process. Updated periodically, it also includes the list of software deliverable products and its associated guideline or standard to maintain or develop the products.

Section 5: Standards, Practices, Conventions, and Metrics

This section includes all the procedures an SQA team member must verify in order to confirm that the software is of high quality. It includes standards, and monitoring and assurance that the software complies with the listed standards. Furthermore, it also identifies conventions, practices, and standards used in defining, collecting, and using software measurement information.

Section 6: Testing

This section identifies all testing requirements not include in the validation and verification process. It describes the methods or techniques used in detecting bugs. It also lists the method of developing test data, as well as the method to monitor resources.

Section 7: SQA Problem Reporting and Resolution

This section describes the procedures and practices followed by the SQA team for tracking, reporting, and resolving issues in software maintenance and development processes, as well as other software issues. It includes the organizational responsibilities required for software implementation.

Section 8: Tools, Techniques, and Methodologies

This section lists all special techniques, tools, and methodologies, as well as their purpose and use, necessary to perform Software Quality Assurance.

Section 10: Code Control

This section describes the facilities and methods used to document, secure, store, and maintain the controlled software versions during the life cycle of the software.

Section 10: Media Control

This section states the facilities and methods used by the SQA team in identifying the media for every computer product. It also includes the documentation on how to store and restore the media, as well as how to protect the physical media from damage, degradation, and unauthorized access.

Section 11: Supplier Control

This section states the assurance of the SQA team that software needed by the group will be from suppliers who meet the requirements.

Section 12: Records Collection, Maintenance, and Retention

This section identifies the methods and facilities used to maintain, safeguard, and assemble the needed documentation for the SQA process. In addition, it also assigns the retention period for each document.

Section 13: Training

This section determines the training activities needed to meet the requirements of the Software Quality Assurance Plan.

Section 14: Risk Management

This section identifies the procedures and methods used in identifying, monitoring, assessing, and controlling risk areas during the software life cycle.

Implementing Software Quality Assurance

Quality assurance systems aim to satisfy the customers. The resources, processes, and procedures keep the organization focused on activities and goals. More often than not, customers reach a high level of satisfaction if the organization developed programs, products, and services that ensure consistent delivery to please customers.

Determine the Goals of the Organization

Quality assurance starts with the definition of job descriptions of employees that relate to the organizational goals of the company. The employees must know the company's vision, mission, values, and their roles in it. The organization must provide thorough orientation to new employees so that they know how they relate to the organization.

Determine Critical Success Factors

The quality assurance system must identify the factors that will make it successful. Such factors may include employee satisfaction, customer support, great product, well-designed production process, technical support, or financial security. The major factors must be able to influence the quality assurance process in a consistent and continuous manner.

Determine External and Internal Users

For the quality assurance system to work, the team must identify the major groups of customers. It is important that the group knows the needs of their customers so that they can develop software products and services that satisfy them. In general, customers can include direct clients, vendors, employees, suppliers, or volunteers.

Gather Customer Feedback

Customer feedback is important to the quality assurance process. By generating consistent feedback from customers, an organization can easily discover and solve problems about quality. It can obtain customer feedback by interviewing the customers in person, by phone and email, and through customer surveys and focus groups.

The organization's customer service representative can call the customers after purchasing the product to ask about customer satisfaction. He can also conduct in-person surveys after work or after product delivery. In addition, the organization can review returned products and customer complaints. The objective of customer feedback is to gather information to improve the quality of the software.

Implement Continuous Improvements

Quality assurance is the same as continuous improvement. From the customer feedback, the organization must make the required changes to its quality assurance methodologies. This means that it must provide more customer service training, leadership development, product process correction, product or service changes, or higher level of staffing. It is important for the organization to study the customer feedback and commit to improve its processes continuously so that it can deliver products and services with the highest quality.

Choose Quality Management Software

The organization must choose quality assurance software to help it implement the quality assurance processes. In addition, the quality assurance software can also help the company improve and maintain its processes.

Determine the Results

In implementing a quality assurance plan, the organization must ensure that it meets its customers' requirements. It will be difficult for the company to produce a positive return on investment if it is not able to meet the requirements of its clients. In addition, the organization may cease to exist if it continuously fails to provide a high level of customer satisfaction.

The organization must ensure that its goals are measurable and that everyone in the company is involved and committed to meets the company goals. In case there is a failure to achieve the goals, each employee must be able to participate in taking the necessary corrective action so that the organization will be able to maintain its customers and generate new ones by providing quality software that meets their requirements.

Chapter 7: Software Reliability Testing

Software reliability testing relates to the ability of the software to function under environmental conditions within a period through testing. It helps discover errors in the software functionality and design.

Software reliability follows a formula. It is:

Probability = # of failing cases / total # of cases under consideration

To test for software reliability, data gathering occurs during the different development stages. Because of restrictions in time and cost, testing may be limited, as well. If there is sufficient information, statistical studies commence using fixed deadlines or dates to handle time constraints. Software design ceases and actual implementation begins. It is important for data gathering to be precise because of time and cost restrictions.

Software Failure Mechanisms

Software failures are due to misinterpretation of software requirements, oversights, ambiguities, or errors. Other causes of software failures include incompetence or carelessness of application developers, unexpected or incorrect software usage, inadequate testing, and other unexpected problems.

Usually, a defect in the software design can cause failures. Failures can occur unexpectedly. In some cases, restarting the software can help fix the problems. However, the reliability of the software does not depend on its life cycle and time. Environmental factors can affect inputs but they cannot affect reliability of the software.

It is impossible to predict software reliability. Identical software components cannot improve software reliability. However, standardized logic structures in software code, if extensively tested and well understood, can improve reliability and maintainability.

Software Reliability Models

There are at least 200 software reliability models available since the 1970s. However, no single model can satisfy the software complexity thus, assumptions and constraints are included to quantify the process. Most models have assumptions, a mathematical function, and factors that relate to software reliability. In most cases, the mathematical function is logarithmic or exponential.

The software modeling techniques fall under two categories: prediction and estimation. Both techniques accumulate and observe failure data and analyze it with statistical inference. However, the prediction model uses historical data and used before the test or development phases. It is able to predict software reliability in the future. On the other hand, the estimation models uses current data and used at a later software life cycle. It can predict software reliability at some future time or at present.

Software Reliability Metrics

Measurement is easy in most engineering fields. However, the same is not true in software engineering. Measurement is frustrating and there is really no good measurement method for software reliability. It is difficult because no one has a good understanding of software. In fact, there is no appropriate measurement method for software reliability unless experts are able to define the aspects related to it.

Currently, there are four categories for software reliability measurement namely, product metrics, project management metrics, process metrics, and fault and failure metrics.

Product Metrics

Software size is a reflection of reliability, development effort, and complexity. Intuitively, the Lines of Code (LOC) measures software size. However, there is no standard method for measurement. Usually, non-executable statement and comments do not count. Only the source code does. This way of counting cannot compare with software written in other programming languages.

The function point metric measures the functionality of software development based on interfaces, inquiries, master files, inputs, and outputs. It estimates software size when functions are already identifiable. It measures business systems but are not scientific.

Complexity, on the other hand, relates directly to software reliability. There are metrics that measure complexity by determining the control structure of the program and simplifying the code graphically.

Lastly, test coverage metrics estimate reliability and fault by testing the software based on the assumption that once a part of software is tested, the software is reliable.

Project Management Metrics

Good management results to good software products. According to research, using inadequate processes can increase costs. The use of better development process, configuration management process, and risk management process can achieve higher reliability.

Process Metrics

According to process metrics, software quality is a direct function of software process. Thus, it is advisable to use process metrics in estimating, monitoring, and improving software quality and reliability through the ISO-9000 certification.

Fault and Failure Metrics

It is the objective of fault and failure metrics to determine when the software is nearing failure-free execution. The collection, summarization, and analysis of the number of faults and failures reported by end users after software delivery are important in achieving the objective. The effectiveness of fault metrics is highly related to the test strategy. If the test strategy does not include the software's full functionality, the software may fail once delivered to clients even though it passes all tests.

Software Reliability Testing Objectives

The primary goal of reliability testing is to ensure the software performs well under certain conditions using its specifications and fixed procedures. Its secondary goal is to search for a structure of repeating failures, number of failures within a certain period, the mean life of the software, and the primary cause of the failure. Lastly, its secondary objective is to check the performance of the software units after pursuing preventive action.

In drafting objectives, it is good to bear in mind that it is important to define software behavior in certain condition. The objectives must consider time constraints and must be feasible.

Importance of Software Reliability Testing

Today, software applications are important in any industry. The various applications make software reliability testing become an essential part of the process. Software reliability testing has become a tool to measure in quantitative and scientific terms the latest software engineering technologies.

In order to improve the process of software development and software performance, assessment of reliability must take place. Software reliability testing is useful for software managers and users. To verify software reliability, it is important to have enough test cases within a specific period for testing to commence. Testing must be able to identify defects that can cause software failure. In general, if software function more often used, it must have a greater number of test cases to ensure that it can run without failure.

Kinds of Software Reliability Testing

Testing includes regression testing, load testing, and feature testing. Regression testing tries to discover new errors, which may result from fixing a previous error. Usually, it occurs after every update or change in the software.

Load testing, on the other hand, aims to verify the software performance under maximum load. In general, software response time may decrease after some amount of workload. For example, a website may undergo load testing to discover how many users it can support simultaneously without any decrease in response time. Lastly, feature testing monitors the software features for any errors or bugs.

How to Measure Software Reliability

The mean time between failures includes the mean time to repair and the mean time to failure. If there is a restriction on operation time, a person can use compressed time accelerations to limit the testing time. The mean time to failure takes into consideration the calendar time, number of on-off cycles, and operating time. If calendar time is the focus, it is advisable to use intensified stress testing.

Software's reliability increases when there are no more bugs or errors discovered. For example, if the mean time between failures is 1000 hours for standard software, the software to be tested must be able to work for 1,000 hours continuously. The mean time to repair is the time needed to fix the error while the mean time to failure is the time difference between two succeeding failures.

Planning the Software Reliability Testing

Reliability testing is more expensive than other kinds of testing. Therefore, it is important to follow the required steps to plan and manage it properly. Planning includes the implementation of the testing process, testing schedule, environment data, test points, and others.

Some problems may become evident when designing test cases. It is possible to choose valid input values on every software field so that testing will be simple. If there are changes in a specific module, it is possible that previous values will not work on the new features. Critical software runs may not be possible with the present test case. As such, it is important to consider various test cases carefully when selecting a particular test case.

Enhancing Software Reliability through Testing

Studies during software design and development can improve software reliability. By performing reliability testing, it is possible to eliminate the software failure mode. It is also important to perform life testing after finishing the software design.

Testing of new software prototypes for failure is important to detect the causes of failure and prescribe actions to fix them. If there are features added to the software, a test case must be prepared in a different way. The Software Quality Assurance team must be able to determine the number of new test cases for the present software version. If a new feature is part of an existing feature, the team can share test cases between the two features. Lastly, the group can combine the test cases of the previous and present versions then record the results.

Evaluation of Software Reliability through Operational Testing

Operational testing checks software performance in an operational environment. However, it is not easy to create an operational environment like in aircraft industries, nuclear industries, etc. It is possible to perform reliability evaluation through reliability growth based prediction and steady state reliability estimation.

In steady state reliability estimation, data from delivered software can predict the reliability of the software's next version. On the other hand, the reliability growth based prediction uses documentation from past test data to observe a trend and predict the next version's reliability.

The prediction and assessment of reliability uses the reliability growth model. Failure data from the software operation serves as input to this model, which can evaluate software reliability. However, it is important to note that there is no best model that can claim to represent the failure process. As such, it is important to select the model based on the predetermined conditions.

Reliability estimation, on the other hand, assumes that somebody will fix the error when discovered. Fixing it will not affect the software reliability and that the fix is accurate.

Chapter 8: Introducing Software Quality Assurance Procedures To An Existing Company

The introduction of the software quality assurance procedures rely on the risks involved and the company's size. If the organization is large and the projects are high-risk, the management must consider a more formal quality assurance process. On the other hand, if the risk is lower, the implementation of quality assurance may be a step-at-a-time procedure. The processes of quality assurance maintain balance with productivity.

If the project or the company is small, an ad-hoc process may be more appropriate. The success of the software development relies on the team leaders and developers. More importantly, there must be enough communications between software testers, managers, customers, and developers. Requirement specifications must be complete, testable, and clear. There must be procedures for design and code reviews, as well as retrospectives. Common approaches used are Agile, Kaizen, and Deming-Shewhart Plan-Do-Check-Act methods.

It is important to evaluate documents, code, specifications, plans, and requirements. To do this, it is necessary to prepare issues lists, checklists, inspection meetings, and walkthroughs. This process is what IT people refer to as verification. On the other hand, validation occurs after verification and includes actual testing of the application. A walkthrough is evaluation in an informal meeting. There is no need to prepare for it.

An inspection is more formal than a walkthrough and attended by at most eight people including a reader, a recorder, and a moderator. Usually, an inspection's subject is a test plan or requirements specification so that the attendees will know the software's problems. The attendees must read the document before attending an inspection so they will find the problems prior to the meeting. It is difficult to prepare for an inspection but it is an effective and least costly way to ensure quality.

Testing Requirements That Must Be Considered

The basis of black box testing is the software's functionality and requirements. A software tester need not be knowledgeable of code or internal design. White box testing, on the other hand, requires knowledge of code. It takes into consideration the code statements, paths, branches, and conditions. Unit testing requires testing of particular code modules or functions. Usually, the application developer performs it because it requires detailed knowledge of the code and program design.

API testing is testing of data exchange or messaging among systems parts. An incremental integration testing tests the application when there is a new functionality, which must be independent to work separately before it can be included in the application. The application programmer or software tester performs this type of testing. An integration testing requires the testing of the various parts of the software in order to know if they work together properly. Functional testing, on the other hand, is a kind of black box testing that focuses on the application's functional requirements. The software testers perform it.

System testing is also another type of black box testing. It includes testing of the general requirements specifications and all the various parts of the software. End-to-end testing, on the other hand, is a macro type of system testing. It includes testing the whole software in various situations that replicates real-world use. Smoke testing or sanity testing is an initial testing to know if the new version is performing well so that major testing can commence. Regression testing retests the application after some modifications or fixes.

Acceptance testing is final testing the software based on customer's specifications. Load testing is software testing under heavy loads in order to find out when the response time of the system fails or degrades. Stress testing, on the other hand, is system functional testing with unusually heavy loads, large complex queries of the database, using large numerical values, and heavy repetition of certain inputs or actions. Performance testing is testing using test or quality assurance plans.

The goal of usability testing depends on the customer or end-user. It uses techniques like surveys, user interviews, and user sessions' video recording. Software testers and developers are not the people to implement usability testing. Install/uninstall testing uses processes to test upgrade, full, or partial install/uninstall of the software. Recovery testing determines how the software can recover in catastrophic instances like hardware failures and crashes. Failover testing is another name for recovery testing.

Security testing tests how the application protects against willful damage, unauthorized access, and the likes. It uses sophisticated testing methods. Compatibility testing tests how the application performs in some environments. Exploratory testing, on the other hand, is an informal and creative testing that does not use any formal test cases or plans. Usually, software testers are new to the application. Ad-hoc testing is almost the same as exploratory testing but the software testers understand the application prior to testing.

Context-driven testing focuses on the software's intended use, culture, and environment. For example, medical equipment software has a different testing approach than a computer game. User acceptance testing determines if the application is satisfactory to the customer or end-user. Comparison testing, on the other hand, compares the software with its competitors.

Alpha testing occurs when the software is almost finished. Usually, end users perform this type of testing. Beta testing is testing when the software is finished and ready for final release. Like alpha testing, this kind of testing is for end users. Finally, mutation testing uses test cases and allows for code changes and retesting using the original test cases to discover software bugs.

Common Problems and Solutions in Developing Software

Software development can encounter common problems like poor user stories or requirements, unrealistic schedule, inadequate testing, featuritis, and miscommunication. Problems can arise if there requirements are incomplete, unclear, not testable, or too general. Furthermore, if the software development has a short timetable, problems can also be evident. If the software does not pass through the testing process, the IT organization will only know of problems if the system crashes or the end users complain.

In addition, problems can arise if the users or customers request for more new functionalities even after the development goals are set. Finally, if there is miscommunication between the programmers and customers, problems are inevitable. If it is an agile project, the problems become evident when it strays away from agile principles.

If there are common problem then there are also common solutions like solid requirements, realistic schedules, adequate testing, sticking to original requirements, and communication. Software requirements must be complete, clear, cohesive, detailed, testable, and attainable. All players concerned must agree upon them. In agile environments, there must be close coordination with end users or customers so that any change in requirement is clear. There must be enough time for design, planning, bug fixing, testing, changes, retesting, and documentation. Each person must not feel burnout during the project.

For testing to be adequate, it must start early. Retesting must occur after each change or fix. There must be enough time for bug fixing and testing. If the end user or customer requests for excessive changes when development has begun, it is important that the project manager explain the consequences. If the change is important, a schedule change is inevitable to accommodate it.

The project manager must manage the expectations of the end users or customer. In an agile environment, the project manager can expect significant change in the initial requirements. There must be a schedule for inspections and walkthroughs. The use of communication tools is important to ensure cooperation and teamwork.

Software Quality Assurance and Software Quality Control in the Workplace

If there is no formal implementation of Software Quality Assurance/Software Quality Control, the quality group can mirror that of an engineering services group. It performs the tasks not done by the development team. It reports to the application development manager. Under this scenario, the manager can instruct the quality assurance personnel to install a load-testing tool and declare him as a performance expert. Although the quality assurance person must perform load testing, it is the job of the software designer/programmer. As such, the software quality assurance/software quality control must be separate from the development team.

Software quality assurance requires the establishment of templates used during reviews. Such templates must have sections for both non-functional and functional requirements. For example, the requirements for performance must be in terms of transaction rates and user population. The use of Traceability Matrix can help in the requirements management. The matrix also encourages the analyst to use individual requirements for cross-referencing.

Software quality assurance verifies that the requirements comply with the templates and that they are not ambiguous. It reviews the risks of non-completion of the non-functional attributes, as well as the Traceability Matrix, to ensure usability of all requirements in other specifications. Software quality assurance can write the test cases, which refer to some of the requirements. It can cross-reference the requirements in the Traceability Matrix.

The interface specification is a requirement if the software is component-based. Software quality assurance must subject the document to verification. It must also subject other lower level specifications to quality assurance if such requirements are critical. Even if there are limited resources for software quality assurance, an IT organization can obtain a good return-on-investment if it pays attention to requirements and interfaces.

Chapter 9: Ensuring Software Quality

Software quality is the delivery of bug-free software within budget and on time. Because quality is subjective, it depends on the customer and his overall influence in the project. A customer can be an end user, a customer contract officer, a customer acceptance tester, a customer manager, a software maintenance engineer, and others. Each customer has his own definition of quality.

A code is good if it works, is secure, bug free, maintainable, and readable. Some companies have standards, which their programmers follow. However, each developer has his own idea about what is best. Standards have different metrics and theories. If there are excessive rules and standards, they can limit creativity and productivity. A design can be functional or internal design.

An internal design is good if the overall structure of the software code is clear, easily modifiable, understandable, and maintainable. It is robust with the capability to log status and with sufficient error handling. Furthermore, the software works as expected. A functional design is good if the software functionality comes from the requirements of the end user and customer. Even an inexperienced user can use the software without reading the user manual or seeking online help.

The software life cycle starts with the conception of the application and commences when the software is no longer used. It includes factors like requirements analysis, initial concept, internal design, functional design, test planning, documentation planning, document preparation, coding, maintenance, testing, integration, retesting, updates, and phase out.

A good software test engineer must possess a test to break attitude, which means that he must be able to focus on the detail in order to ensure that the application is of good quality. He must be diplomatic and tactful so that he can maintain a good relationship with the programmers, the customers, and the managements.

It is helpful if he has previous experience on software development so that he understands the whole process deeply. A good software test engineer is able to appreciate the point of view of the programmers. He must have good judgment skills to be able to determine critical or high-risk application areas that require testing.

A good quality assurance engineer also shares the same qualities with a good software test engineer. Furthermore, he must understand the whole process of software development and the organizations' goals and business approach. He must possess understanding of all sides of issues in order to communicate effectively with everyone concerned. He must be diplomatic and patient, especially in the early stages of the quality assurance process. Lastly, he must be able to detect problems during inspections and reviews.

Qualities of a Good Quality Assurance or Test Manager

A good manager must be familiar with the process of software development and must be enthusiastic and promote positivity in the team. He must be able to increase productivity by promoting teamwork and cooperation between quality assurance, software, and test engineers. If the processes require improvements, he must be diplomatic in ensuring smooth implementation of such changes.

He must be able to withstand pressure and offer the right feedback about quality issues to the other managers. He must be able to hire and keep the right personnel. He must possess strong communication skills to deal with everyone concerned in the process. Lastly, he must stay focused and be able to hold meetings.

Importance of Documentation in Quality Assurance

If the team is large, it is more useful to have the proper documentation for efficient communication and management of projects. Documentation of quality assurance practices is necessary for repeatability. Designs, specifications, configurations, business rules, test plans, code changes, bug reports, test cases, and user manuals must have proper documentation. A system of documentation is necessary for easy obtaining and finding of information.

Each project has its own requirements. If it is an agile project, the requirements may change and evolve. Thus, there is no need for detailed documentation. However, it is useful to document user stories. Documentation on the software requirements describes the functionality and properties of the software. It must be clear, reasonably detailed, complete, attainable, cohesive, and testable. It may be difficult to organize and determine the details but there are tools and methods that are available.

It is important to exercise care in documenting the requirements of the project's customer, who may be an outside or in-house personnel, an end user, a customer contract officer, a customer acceptance tester, a customer manager, a sales person, or a software maintenance engineer. If the project did not meet the expectations, any of these customers can slow down the project.

Each organization has its own way of handling requirements. If the project is an agile project, the requirements are in the user stories. On the other hand, for other projects, the requirements are in the document. Some organizations may use functional specification and high-level project plans. In every requirement, documentation is important to help software testers to make test plans and perform testing. Without any significant documentation, it is impossible to determine if the application meets the user expectations.

Even if the requirements are not testable, it is still important to test the software. The test results must be oriented towards providing information about the risk levels and the status of the application. It is significant to have the correct testing approach to ensure success of the project. In an agile project, various approaches can use methods that require close cooperation and interaction among stakeholders.

Chapter 10; How To Develop And Run Software Testing

To develop the steps for software testing, it is necessary to consider the following.

First, it is important to get the requirements, user stories, internal design, functional design, and any other information that can help with the testing process.

Second, testing must have budget and schedule.

Third, it must have personnel with clear responsibilities.

Fourth, there must be project context to determine testing approaches, scope, and methods.

Fifth, identification of limitations and scope of tests is necessary in order to set priorities.

Sixth, testing must include methods and approaches applicable.

Seventh, it must have the requirements to determine the test environment.

Eighth, it must have requirements for testing tools.

Ninth, it is important to determine the data requirements for testing input.

Tenth, identification of labor requirements and tasks are important.

Eleventh, it must determine milestones, timelines, and schedule estimates.

Twelfth, testing must include error classes, boundary value analysis, and input equivalence classes, when needed.

Thirteenth, it must have a test plan and documents for approvals and reviews.

Fourteenth, testing must determine test scenarios and cases.

Fifteenth, it must include reviews, approvals of test cases, inspections, approaches, and scenarios.

Sixteenth, there must be testing tools and test environment, user manuals, configuration guides, reference documents, installation guides, test tracking processes, archiving and logging processes, and test input data.

Seventeenth, it must include software releases,

The Test Plan

A test plan is a document, which includes scope, objectives, and focus of the software testing activity. To prepare it, it is important to consider the efforts needed to validate the software's acceptability. The test plan must help even those people who are not part of the test group. Testing must be thorough but not very detailed.

The test plan can include the following: the title, the software version number, the plan's revision history, table of contents, the intended audience, the goal of testing, the overview of the software, relevant documents, legal or standards requirements, identifier and naming standards, and requirements for traceability. The test plan must also include overall project organization, test organization, dependencies and assumptions, risk analysis of the project, focus and priorities of testing, limitations and scope, test outline, data input outline, test environment, analysis of test environment validity, configuration and setup of test environment, and processes for software migration among other things.

A test case includes the input, event, or action plus its expected result in order to know if software's functionality is working as planned. It contains test case identifier, objective, test case name, test setup, requirements for input data, steps, and expected results. The details may differ, depending on the project context and organization. Some organizations handle test cases differently. Most of them use less-detailed test scenarios for simplicity and adaptability of test documentation. It is important to develop test cases because it is possible to detect problems and errors in the software through them.

When a Bug is Discovered

If the software has a bug, the programmers must fix it. The software must undergo retesting after the resolution of the error. Regression testing must be able to check that the solutions performed were not able to create more problems within the application. A system for problem tracking must be set up so it becomes easier to perform the retesting. There are various software tools available to help the quality assurance team.

In tracking the problems, it is good to consider the following: complete information about the bug, bug identifier, present bug status, software version number, how the bug was discovered, specifics about environment and hardware, test case information, bug description, cause of the bug, fix description, retesting results, etc. There must be a reporting process so that the appropriate personnel will know about the errors and fixes.

A configuration management includes the various processes used to coordinate, control, and track requirements, code, problems, documentation, designs, change requests, tools, changes made, and person who made the changes. If the software has many bugs, the software tester must report them and focus on critical bugs. Because this problem can affect the schedule, the software tester must inform the managers and send documentation in order to substantiate the problem.

The decision to stop testing is difficult to do, especially for complex applications. In some cases, complete testing is not possible. Usually, the decision to stop testing considers the deadlines, the degree of test cases completion, the depletion of the test budget, the specified coverage of code, the reduction of the bug rate, and the ending of alpha or beta testing periods. If there is not enough time to perform thorough testing, it is important to focus the testing on important matters based on risk analysis. If the project is small, the testing can depend on risk analysis again.

In some cases, there are organizations that are not serious about quality assurance. For them, it is important to solve problems rather than prevent problems. Problems regarding software quality may not be evident. Furthermore, some organizations reward people who fix problems instead of incentivizing prevention of problems. Risk management includes actions that prevent things from happening. It is a shared responsibility among stakeholders. However, there must be a point person who is primarily responsible for it. In most cases, the responsibility falls on the quality assurance personnel.

Chapter 11: Deciding When To Release The Software To Users

In most projects, the decision to release the software depends on the timing of the end testing. However, for most applications, it is difficult to specify the release criteria without using subjectivity and assumptions. If the basis of the release criteria is the result of a specific test, there is an assumption that this test has addressed all the necessary software risks.

For many projects, this is impossible to do without incurring huge expenses. Therefore, the decision is actually a leap of faith. Furthermore, most projects try to balance cost, timeliness, and quality. As such, testing cannot address the balance of such factors when there is a need to decide on the release date.

Usually, the quality assurance or test manager decides when to release the software. However, this decision involves various assumptions. First, the test manager understands the considerations, which are significant in determining the quality of the software to justify release. Second, the quality of the software may not balance with cost and timeliness. In most organization, there is not enough definition for sufficient quality. Thus, it becomes very subjective and may vary from day to day or project to project.

The release criteria must consider the sales goals, deadlines, market considerations, legal requirements, quality norms of the business segment, programming and technical considerations, expectations of end users, internal budget, impact on the other projects, and a host of other factors. Usually, the project manager must know all these factors.

Because of the various considerations, it may not be possible for the quality assurance manager or test manager to decide the release of the software. However, he may be responsible in providing inputs to the project manager, who makes the release decision. If the project or the organization is small, the decision to release the software rests on the project manager or the product manager. For larger organizations or projects, there must be a committee to decide when to release the software.

If the software requirements change continuously, it is important for all stakeholders to cooperate from the beginning so that they all understand how the change in requirements may affect the project. They may decide on alternate strategies and test plans in advance. It is also beneficial to the project if the initial design of the software can accommodate changes later on. A well-documented code makes it easier for programmers to make the necessary changes.

It is also good to use rapid prototyping if possible so that customers will not make more requests for changes because they are sure of their requirements from the very beginning. The initial schedule of the project must allow extra lead-time for these changes. If possible, all changes must be in the "Phase 2" of the software version. It is important that only easily implemented requirements must be in the project.

The difficult ones must be in the future versions. The management and the customers must know about costs, inherent risks, and scheduling impacts of big changes in the requirements. If they know about the challenges, they can decide whether to continue with the changes or not.

There must be balance between expected efforts with the effort to set up automated testing for the changes. The design of the automated test scripts must be flexible. Its focus must be on aspects of application, which will remain unchanged. The reduction of the appropriate effort for the risk analysis of the changes can be through regression testing.

The design of the test cases must be flexible. The focus must be on ad-hoc testing and not on detailed test cases and test plans. If there is a continuous request for changes in the requirements, it is unreasonable to expect that requirements will remain stable and pre-determined. Thus, it may be appropriate to use approaches for agile development.

It is difficult to determine if software has significant hidden or unexpected functionality. It also indicates that the software development process has deeper problems. The functionality must be removed if does not serve any purpose to the software because it may have unknown dependencies or impacts. If not removed, there must be a consideration for the determination of regression testing needs and risks. The management must know if there are significant risks caused by the unexpected functionality.

The implementation of quality assurance processes is slow over time because the stakeholders must have a consensus. There must be an alignment of processes and organizational goals. As the organization matures, there will be an improvement on productivity. Problem prevention will be the focus. There will be a reduction of burnout and panics. There will be less wasted effort and more improved focus.

The processes must be efficient and simple to prevent any "Process Police" mentality. Furthermore, quality assurance processes promote automated reporting and tracking thereby minimizing paperwork. However, in the short run, implementation may be slow. There will be more days for inspections, reviews, and planning but less time for handling angry end users and late night fixing of errors.

If the growth of the IT organization is very rapid, fixed quality assurance processes may be impossible. Thus, it is important to hire experienced people. The management must prioritize issues about quality and maintain a good relationship with the customers. Every employee must know what quality means to the end user.

Chapter 12: Using Automated Testing Tools

If the project is small, learning and implementing the automated testing tools may not be worth it. However, these automated testing tools are important for large projects. These tools use a standard coding language like Java, ruby, python, or other proprietary scripting language. In some cases, it is necessary to record the first tests for the generation of the test scripts. Automated testing is challenging if there are continuous changes to the software because a change in test code is necessary every time there is a new requirement. In addition, the analysis and interpretation of results can be difficult.

Data driven or keyword driven testing is common in functional testing. The maintenance of actions and data is easy through a spreadsheet. The test drivers read the information for them to perform the required tests. This strategy provides more control, documentation, development, and maintenance of test cases. Automated tools can include code analyzers, coverage analyzers, memory analyzers, load/performance test tools, web test tools, and other tools.

A test engineer, who does manual testing, determines if the application performs as expected. He must be able to judge the expected outcome. However, in an automated test, the computer judges the test outcome. A mechanism must be present for the computer to compare automatically between the actual and expected outcomes for every test scenario. If the test engineer is new to automated testing, it is important that he undergo training first.

Proper planning and analysis are important in selecting and using an automated tool for testing. The right tool must be able to test more thoroughly than manual methods. It must test faster and allow continuous integration. It must also reduce the tedious manual testing. The automation of testing is costly. However, it may be able to provide savings in the long term.

Choosing the Appropriate Test Environment

There is always a tradeoff between cost and test environment. The ultimate scenario is to have a collection of test environments, which mirror exactly all possible usage, data, network, software, and hardware characteristics that the software can use. For most software, it is impossible to predict all environment variations. Furthermore, for complex and large systems, it is extremely expensive to duplicate a live environment.

The reality is that decisions on the software environment characteristics are important. Furthermore, the choice of test environments takes into consideration logistical, budget, and time constraints. People with the most technical experience and knowledge, as well as with the deep understanding of constraints and risks, make these decisions. If the project is low risk or small, it is common to take the informal approach. However, for high risk or large projects, it is important to take a more formalize procedure with many personnel.

It is also possible to coordinate internal testing with efforts for beta testing. In addition, it is possible to create built-in automated tests upon software installation by users. The tests are able to report information through the internet about problems and application environment encountered. Lastly, it is possible to use virtual environments.

The Best Approach to Test Estimation

It is not easy to find the best approach because it depends on the IT organization, the project, as well as the experience of the people involved. If there are two projects with the same size and complexity, the right test effort for life-critical medical software may be very large compared to a project involving an inexpensive computer game. The choice of a test estimation approach based on complexity and size may be applicable to a project but not to the other one.

The implicit risk context approach caters to a quality assurance manager or project manager, who uses risk context with past personal experiences to allocate resources for testing. The risk context assumes that each project is similar to the others. It is an experience-based intuitive guess.

The metrics-based approach, on the other hand, uses past experiences on different projects. If there is already data from a number of projects, the information is beneficial in future test planning. For each new project, the basis of adjustment of required test time is the available metrics. In essence, this is not easy to do because it is judgment based on historical experience.

The test-work breakdown approach decomposes the testing tasks into smaller tasks to estimate testing with a reasonable accuracy. It assumes that the breakdown of testing tasks is predictable and accurate and that it is feasible to estimate the testing effort. If the project is large, this is not feasible because there is a need to extend testing time if there are many bugs. In addition to, there is a need to extend development time.

The iterative approach is for large test projects. An initial rough estimate is necessary prior to testing. Once testing begins and after finishing a small percentage of testing work, there is a need to update the testing estimate because testers have already obtained additional knowledge of the issues, risks, and software quality. There is also a need to update test schedules and plans. After finishing a larger percentage of testing work, the testing estimate requires another update. The cycle continues until testing ends.

The percentage-of-development approach requires a quick way of testing estimation. If the project has 1,000 hours of estimated programming effort, the

IT firm usually assigns a 40% ratio for testing. Therefore, it will allot 400 hours for testing. The usefulness of this approach depends on risk, software type, personnel, and complexity level.

In an agile software development approach, the test estimate is unnecessary if the project uses pure test-driven development although it is common to mix some automated unit tests with either automated or manual functional testing. By the nature of agile-based projects, they are not dependent on testing efforts but on the construction of the software.

Conclusion

Thank you again for purchasing this book!

I hope this book was able to help you to understand the concepts of Software Quality Assurance.

The next step is to apply what you learned from this book to your work.

Finally, if you enjoyed this book, please take the time to share your thoughts and post a review on Amazon. It'd be greatly appreciated!

Thank you and good luck!